Girl, Discovered

Girl, Discovered

Poems by

Frances Ruhlen McConnel

© 2019 Frances Ruhlen McConnel. All rights reserved. This material may not be reproduced in any form, published, reprinted, recorded, performed, broadcast, without the express written consent of Frances Ruhlen McConnel. All such actions are strictly prohibited by law.

Cover design by Shay Culligan

ISBN: 978-1-949229-81-3

Kelsay Books
Aldrich Press
www.kelsaybooks.com

This book is for my first family:

Deborah Ruhlen, 1905-1967; Harold Ruhlen, 1906-1965;
Agnes Smith, 1873-1964; Russell Ruhlen, 1942-2011;
and Raymond Ruhlen, 1939.

Acknowledgments

The author gratefully acknowledges the publishers of journals and anthologies in which some of these poems first appeared, sometimes in slightly different forms:

Poetry Northwest: "Chicken Killer"

The Cimarron Review: "Circus"

Assay: "Grail," "Six Bold Turtles"

Crab Creek Review: "Souvenir from a Radioactive Town"

Mudlark and *Mischief, Caprice, and Poetic Strategies (*Red Hen Press Anthology): "We Dream of Heroes"

Bellowing Ark and *Poemeleon:* "In the Garden, My Mother Invokes Wordsworth"

Mosaic: "Young Lovers at Crow Creek Mine*"*

Tyee: "Solstice at Hidden Lake"

I could watch! I could watch!
I saw the separateness of all things!
My heart lifted up with the great grasses;
The weeds believed me, and the nesting birds.
There were clouds making a rout of shapes crossing
a windbreak of cedars,
And a bee shaking drops from a rain-soaked honeysuckle.
The worms were delighted as wrens.
And I walked, I walked through the light air;
I moved with the morning.

  —Theodore Roethke, "A Field of Light"

I went to the wood and got it;
I sat me down to look for it
And brought it home because I couldn't find it.

  —*The Real Mother Goose*, "The Thorn"

Contents

Circus	13
Grail	16
Souvenir from a Radioactive Town	19
Recital	21
Family	24
Camping out	26
Chicken Killer	27
Wild Persimmons	29
All Together Now	31
Pastoral with Stars	33
To be Eleven	36
We Dream of Heroes	37
Six Bold Turtles	39
Mummy	41
In the Garden, My Mother Invokes Wordsworth	44
Ode to a Parka	46
Solstice at Hidden Lake	48
Young Lovers at Crow Creek Mine	49

Circus

Death has the face of a clown,
white as moths with a red mouth
turned down like a dill pickle
and enormous tears on his cheek,

beckoning to us with one hand
while the other plucks a bouquet
of yellow paper roses
out of the nowhere he came from.

The short clown with floppy feet
who hits him upside the head
with a rubber chicken and chases him off
is no angel, though you might wish so.

Or he's one of the fallen ones
that Death, disguised as the devil,
dragged with him from heaven
maybe in the same jalopy

he's come back in and when
he opens the door clowns pour out
and run as if a giant hand at any moment
could snatch them up and pop them

into an enormous mouth.
When he comes right up
to our bleacher, our little brother
buries his face in our dad's belly;

but I'm not scared, I brag,
jammed between my mom
and big brother, except of the crowd's
crashing, headless laughter.

And aren't circuses meant to scare you,
with lions who gnaw at the air
as they slink, ranting,
onto their star-spangled stands?

And when the acrobats fling
themselves into nothingness
and snatch each other back,
you have to crane your neck

and look up into the dark caverns
of the tent roof which sags ominously
with pent-up rain, some of which
drops into your hair and even

your eyes. Then drum sticks begin to throb
and the tight-rope walker makes the line
swing wildly under him and you can't
look or you might bring him down.

When we come out into the dark,
stars are popping out above us
and puddles we slosh through.
And the ancient Pierce Arrow

heaves and grinds and belches
in the grip of mud, smoke rising,
until the spud our dad jammed
into the open radiator mouth

in place of a missing cap
explodes onto the windshield
in what looks like mashed potatoes,
and we all shriek and then laugh,

a car-full of clowns
under the somersaulting constellations:
I'll take that for my funeral, write it down, Sir,
right there on the bottom line.

Grail

1. What Was Lost

The ocean has long since run through the pewter cup
I lost in waves one summer trip
when I squatted on the brilliant beach
pouring the Atlantic into the Atlantic,
scooping cups of sand over my knees.

I dipped shells for my ears and shells for my hair
and shirts and dresses of silver water.
Filling my cup with the salt of your teasing,
the thud of your feet as you rescued my brother
from the blistering bite of sand fleas, Father,

I leaned so long on the edge of the earth,
sand sucked my toes and cup and ocean swirled
through my hands. With sunburn like sand under
my lashes, I fell from your arms and this water
to cry in the weight and lift of your wake.

The conches are shouting the words of my panic.
I cup my hands and the sea pours out and in.
Sands that leak through my fingers glint
in salt and in tears with the shimmer of metal.
Oh, Father, a childhood's a lost and lonely vessel.

2. What Was Left Out

The rented beach cabin, its bleached wooden steps,
linoleum floor.

Explosion of sun filling the sky, making white sand glow,
Jacksonville sand.

Shelf of water above her, endless white runners stroking in.

She'll be careful, mother and grandmother argue.
It's her cup. Her father, growling: *You know she'll lose it.*
She begs, *Please, please.*
Her cup, birth gift from her father's distant parents,
the first girl grandchild,
her engraved name and date she couldn't yet read,
but had rubbed almost out with her thumb. Dented cup,
banged on high chairs, tables.

The seventh wave smashing in, upending her,
wanting her cup, taking her cup.
Her looming father. Being snatched up, spanked,
dropped onto her cot
to lie with her face to the wall.

Let her be, her father chides the womenfolk. *She was warned.*
Her brothers pushed away. But once in a while a soft hand
whisks across back or shoulder.

Soon laughter zings around the room. Dishes clatter.
Smells of sauerkraut, grilling hot dogs.

But she curls herself tighter, cherishing the tears
of her loss as she is meant to do.
And then bitterness comes bubbling up:
for smacks instead of kisses; instead of hugs, exile.
Outrage, shame, self-pity, protest.
A jangle of feelings; her soul dividing itself.

Consciousness.

Postscript: Her father died on her 24th birthday; her nana
3 months earlier; her mother 2 years later.
Her brothers in distant states.
World become myth.
Black hole in the heart of the Milky Way.

Souvenir from a Radioactive Town

Oak Ridge, Tennessee, For Hank. and Debbie.

Did he plant it in her?
Did he carry it through those gates
that allowed no one in or out without a badge?
Was she right when she said
such small dust the men walked through

was nothing compared to that glorious blast
and its towering dust that we saw
in living color on our field trip
to the Atomic Energy Museum.

The blinding shimmer of that blast
that we owned a piece of—our whole town—
hadn't we made it happen, that fire-storm, slow-motion cloud,
the way all of Hershey, PA, creates chocolate?

On the way back to buses, we fisted
the plastic-sealed, radioactive dimes
they handed out, that set off the Geiger counter
at the door like a Chinese Cracker.

That was the way we laughed,
in sputtering explosions, peeling and dropping
souvenir dimes into our jeans pockets
where Mom, without even a Geiger counter,

found them before she did the wash,
found and dropped them into her apron pocket,
that and whatever doodads Dad picked up at work.
Then she shook out the dust, its little puffs of nothingness,

shook it from his pants cuffs, his lap creases.
Was that the way he planted it in her,
that dust with its invisible seeds of nothingness,
was that how it got in, even without a badge?

Recital

1. Tap Shoes

Hooves of metal, clip-clopping,
You have to learn to make them tappety-tap.
Every step announces you.

Tap forward, tappety back.
Shuffle-clink sideways.
Pick up the scratchy purple rope,
thick as a baby rattler:
Skip-skipping, three sequined girls on stage,
slim, plumper, plumpest.
I check to see if I'm still
the one in the middle.

Heavy shoes not like our ballet slippers—
So tight your feet puff up on top,
So light you'd float unless
you were a chub like me.

Earthbound, I trip,
catch myself, frown.
Then *flash those pearlies*
and ye shall be forgiven.
So says our master.

On taps if you stumble, CLUNK
you add clankety clank.

Three girls in sequined baby bonnets,
Rappety, swish, rappety rap rap.

Cymbals clash. A concert of cymbals.
The air jangling behind us.

Our mouths made coy,
Our eyes trying out *sparkle*.
Tippity-tip, rackety-rack- rack,
cloppety clop, stumpety-stump.
Then: one, two, three, all bow together.

2. Bee Sting

Who or what was to blame—the recital, an event she dreaded worse than the dentist? The ballet class itself or her parents for making her take it? Or Dr. Diamond who prescribed it for her weak ankles? Or the sequined costumes, sewn by a neighbor across the way, Patricia's mom? It surely wasn't her fault for running barefoot across lawn and field to pick up the outfit the morning of the recital—summers, she always went barefoot. And not the fault of wildflowers scattered through the grass—fire pea vetch, clover, bachelor buttons and buttercups. Nor the poor bee, minding its own business when she tromped on it. Plus, it died in the process.

She shook her foot, *ouch, ouch, ouch;* then plopped down to pluck out the stinger, but couldn't see it for the dirt. So she spit on it to make mud and hopped home where her mom and nana tut-tutted as they washed her foot and slathered it with wet baking soda. And she danced anyway. It is not known if she argued to get out of the performance, but gave in to her family's urging to be brave. Or if they'd pitied her and said she could stay home, but she said she had to for the threesome—Patsy, Patricia, and herself.

She will remember the tap part, with the other girls at her side, the silly sequined duck-bill caps, and the stiff purple jump-rope, so rough it could give you splinters. (It had taken team coaxing from teachers and parents to get her even to try to skip rope and tap at the same time—she who couldn't run into a playground's spinning rope without tripping.) She'll remember the music of their taps, like percussion instruments. But she won't remember the ballet part—the pliés, the dégagés—her clumsiness on stage for all to see. Mostly what she will remember is afterwards: her father cutting off the ballet slipper (good riddance!); her foot swollen into a giant radish. And how her brothers were clearly awed, in spite of their teasing. No fault. No blame.

Family

In that house, the girls and boys were even-steven:

A boy cat and a girl dog; two brothers and a dad;
sister, mom, and mom's mom.

The grown-ups were like a totem pole.
The children were like a skirmish.

Stop it, stop it, she cries, over and over.
Stop it, yourself! Big Brother bops her on the bean

to shut her up before anybody notices.
She squinches her eyes and speeds up her chant.

He could have her thumb pulled back to her wrist
or just be teasing. *Stop it.* Sometimes, a threat

and sometimes almost a prayer.
She'd sing it like Peggy Lee if she could.

Mom will be busy in the kitchen with Nana,
steam rising from the big pot,

like autumn mist off a pond,
their faces serene as water lilies.

Then she'll turn to Little Brother for Revenge.
She'll blow the powder off his moth-wings.

She crushes an Oreo down to its black and white atoms.
Then, with the crumbs, she draws constellations,

naming them with his many names—his pet name,
the full name their dad uses; his baby name

from before he was born, animal names:
donkey, piggy, baboon, and so forth.

Then, one by one, she knocks the stars from the skies,
sending them flying or popping them onto her tongue.

Clouds fly across his vision until it is night, only night,
Come back, she begs, suddenly sorry. *Come back.*

And at once his gaze brightens and he whispers
I have X Ray eyes. I can see your undies. I can see your liver.

I can see right through you. In spite of herself,
she shudders. She protests, as always,

there's no such thing. But he smirks,
David to her Goliath, some mythic hero

to her basilisk. Her logic is nothing to his magic.
Stop it, she growls like their cat; grows claws.

Someone better start paying attention from the stove,
before someone pays attention from his evening paper.

Then there will be exile to their shared room
where lawlessness reigns, even if only in whispers

and mute torments, the family riven until dinner is served
and innocence with clean faces and hands restored.

Camping out

After we wash our plastic dishes in lake water,
when flies hush to mosquito purr and pine
chunks sputter red and white, we kids, drained
as the sky of sizzle, bank our coals in the flames' hiss.
All day we fished and rode logs in Lake Watts Bar,
while minnows nibbled the backs of our boney knees.

The taste of muddy water lies in our mouths
thin and flat. Our hands smell salty of gills.
We hear the hoot of the whip-poor-will
moving away, loons chortling.
A shiver goes through me—fear of the fire going out.

Our folks are asleep or silent; beached
on the bank of my brother's body, our dog pants.
Above, a million or so stars dance
with our fire's sparks. I flutter down, alone. I am looking up
into a lake as deep as the bottomless spring
of childhood myth. *Whip-poor-will,* the ripple

flares to enclose us as bubbles blow
from our lips. We are falling away
from earth's shadow into black sky.
We splash out the world and sleep.

Chicken Killer

The golden bloody chick
lay among dusty strawberries,
its neck twisted into a crook
Daisy took in her jaws and shook

until its black eye grew wide
as cedar boughs at dusk.
The down that tickled her tongue
burst soft in my breath

and I saw beyond the garden
the neighbor chasing our dog
who pell-melled into the bushes,
her whole mouth dancing.

Once my brother and I went charging
up to the Seppis' chicken wire.
We banged the soft, erupting
bodies with handfuls of pebbles.

Stuck with gobs of guano,
feathers drummed in our hair
and Papa, yelling, *"Heathens!"*
chased us down the lawn

where the Seppis' bristling shepherd
sped from the edge of azaleas
and tenderly captured his leg.
We yelped with sudden joy

and, phantoms, hung from the bed
as Mama bandaged his ankle.
Our criminal hands stank of hens
and our pockets were warm as eggs.

I nestle the half-grown chick
Into black depths of our cellar,
hiding from Papa the feathers
trailed by the child and the dog

as we ran down the neighbor's lawn
where I dreamed that violent summer
he stabbed me with his shining fork
and ate me, drumstick and all.

Wild Persimmons

Persimmons thud down from the trees:
by day it's us, by night possums
shaking the branches.

Green fruit puckers our mouths like alum.
Ripe ones we eat hanging our heads down
so juices can run free.

The shape of the seeds is cunning as sculpture.
It is mostly seed—seed, a shred of flesh,
and rusty syrup with a bite.

Little brother, we are crouched under
the decaying trestle that arcs a small ravine
in woods near our house,

crouched Indian style, licking sticky fingers,
listening to footsteps above us—
school kids hurrying home

to Oreos and milk, making the bridge's old bones
rattle. Sometimes, looking up, we can see
pink panties under the girls' skirts.

Spies that we are, we've made a truce
from our bicker. We've stamped
to a black corpse the fire

we set in a circle of stones and danced around,
beating out war whoops
with the palms of our hands.

Kiddo, are you thinking as I am of the big boy's
witching wand, that gave up its white juice
if yanked, an act less carnal than agrarian—

squeezing milk from a Holstein's pink teat—
and was, for some reason, hilarious.
Can I guess how this knowledge
will make me appetite's slave at fifteen?

Can you guess how you'll be just the opposite—
a tightly sheathed pip with an edge of bitter,
a sputter of sweet.

All Together Now

We lie on our backs in rows on the cold gym floor
of Elm Grove Elementary, while our gym teacher
guides among us a woman in a business suit
carrying a clipboard where she makes notes,
saying to us, one by one: "Okay, you breathe now."
"You, next," using her pencil as a pointer, frowning
in disbelief. And she's headed down my row.

How were we supposed to breathe?
I try to practice but there's a boulder on my chest.
I feign sleep, but hear their steps stop.
"Your turn, yes, you with the squinched eyes."
So I stiffen up and drag full into my lungs
like a swimmer. "Sad," she says, passing on.
And our gym teacher clucks his tongue in agreement.

Dismay buzzes around in my head. Ten years old
and no one's ever taught me how to breathe?
Not even the doctor who thumped me on the butt
to make me gulp in my first mouth of air—all wrong.
For now the lady with the taboo tap, tap,
of her heels on our new gym floor—is saying
we must breathe from our stomachs.

Our what? I moan. Our stomachs were also
made for breathing? I haven't heard of yoga,
though I've heard from my Southern grandmother:
Suck in your stomach and put some color on!
which seems not to be about breath,
but about grit, or possibly posture.

I'm known as a student willing to please,
but rebellion rises. Why should I let one
of the crucial things my body does without orders
be put in the reins of will-power? When a boy hisses,
"That lady's crazy dumb," instead of *takes one to know one*
what I think is something like *Right on, brother!*

And when she says, "Let's try again; remember,
from the stomach," and our gym teacher calls
with great cheer, "All together now!" for the first time
in my school career, I refuse to cooperate.

Later, walking up the hill home, I looked at dogwoods
and lilacs blooming in people's yards, pea plants
in their gardens, and thought how they breathed
not just through leaves, but with their whole bodies—
flower, stem, trunk, root. I thought of the blow
of humpback whales, inhaling and exhaling oceans,
the pulsating stars. And even the universe
that all our lives had been blowing itself out
into the nothingness, would one day
it get a command to suck it all back?

Soon I'd be home where everyone, even Nana,
breathed as usual, without effort—leaving out
the part about Mom's cigarette cough,
my brother's asthma, Dad's bout with TB—
I skipped, panting, home, not giving a good goddamn.

Pastoral with Stars

In July after supper the day is still long.
Doors are open for a breeze and inside-light
shudders on, filling the bodies of the houses
with pulse. Soon radio voices seep out
like messages from outer space.

Outside-light shrinks step by step across the sky.
The chinaberry tree throws the tarot-tower
of its shadow across garden and porch
where their guardian-spirit grandmother is but
a white blur and soft crackle of newspaper fan.

Dark corners of the yard unfold
fireflies' sleight of hand. A screech owl
wickers at some scurry in the bushes, comes down
like the boom of a summer storm. And it's night.

The three children's backs prickle
from grass-blades damp in the sultry air,
their arms stretched out as if to catch themselves
from falling off the earth's spin.

The youngest thinks himself Alexander the Great,
a boy all night on a ship's deck learning the paths
to steer through constellations
so he might uncover the world's secrets.

The girl wants to fall into the Milky Way, her hair
a Catherine Wheel of light, wants to *be*
a constellation, a new one to send the Zodiac
into a wobble so that no one's life
fits anymore its what-is-to-be.

The eldest feels himself pressed to earth
by the weight of the dome of stars so that
he might sink straight through to the magma
of earth's core and burst out anywhere,
mightier than the laws of nature.

And then the grandeur of their thoughts melts away
and all three give themselves up to night's rapture,
the black emptiness between dreams.
They are dizzy, but unafraid, even of the Looming—
Unreachable, more powerful than any god.

Perhaps a psychic could see something rise
from their heads like the steam of one's breath
in winter--ghost of their longings.
The lostness of it all, orphaned souls beneath
vast space with Time tumbling through it.
And what are they but tumblers, too, with nothing,
perhaps, that thinks of them in these far heavens?

But frogs down at the creek don't care--a steady,
careless palaver with fate. Nor crickets
in their psalms. And, every so often,
the slap of a hand at a mosquito brings them back
to themselves, that solid smack of flesh.

And always stars, silent as stilled gongs,
yet continuing to shiver. And what is this
hollow roar the three feel in their sapling bones—
a surf tossing them like shells in its wake?
Momentous, huge, more yearning than threat,

starting up again their dreams—the edge
of something swinging around, a spaceship, perhaps,
with a million dazzling windows, coming to fetch them,
if they can do what their teasing Nana tells them
and hold their mouths just right.

To be Eleven

It haunts me. Sitting, back to the cold tub-side, finding my feet suddenly almost touching the faucet; could I turn on the Hot with my toes? But no more baptisms of my whole wiggly self, going down under into a different realm, my face covered with a clinging washcloth in some kind of rite: Rebirth? And now my browns and my pinks are scrawled with fat black hairs like the backs of my dad's hands. And sometimes the rank smell of me! Not just Earth's clean dirt to scrub off, but something stuck to the lid of a kitchen garbage pail. It haunts me, the shock and the question: Where did it come from, like some old sin, this werewolfness of me waiting to spring forth?

We Dream of Heroes

Deep in a bramble-bush of stars,
we curl, quivering. A screech owl
wickers above us, her talons
lift what might be our fluttering hearts aloft
to the hollow in the great white spire
of the dead pine where her chicks
open their black throats. In our mouths,
a taste of dying campfires. On our backs
the harsh rasp of sunburn.

We dream of that hero, our father,
that Maker of Bombs, Hank Ruhlen,
who jacked up the corner of the shed
that was listing toward Lake Watts Bar
and dropped it on his foot.
We're dreaming of his three toes,
black as talons, bones shattered
like coke bottles under truck wheels;
how all he said was "Gol-darn it!"

Fish doze now in the arm bones of pines
since they raised the water at Watts Bar Dam.
Mud sleeps in the cabin, mud oozing slow
as smoke from shit, as Mom said
her Pa used to say. Who maybe
learned it from his Pa,
who gave his grandkids coffee,
including the baby (our mother),
hardly before she was weaned,
coffee mud-thick with sugar and fresh cream.
Coffee, he claimed, kept him alive
in the Union prison, when food ran out.

But maybe the shit off which
smoke steamed so slow in the saying
was the hot shit of fear
dropped in the dewy dawn
before the Battle of Shiloh,
where soldiers like exiled kings
fell to kiss the fetid ground and all day
guns racketed from the banks
of the old wild Tennessee,
strolling through under these blood-warm lakes.

Oh, memories of memories like the winking of fireflies.
Oh, whip-poor-will—*Caprimulgus vociferous*—
we wish on your first call at dusk
("Cuck-rhip-oor-ree")
to be like that hero, our father, who fought in no war
except the one against his sons and daughter,
but stoic as a man in a lab-coat,
gave up his life to Uranium 235
and the plant run by Watts Bar Dam kilowatts.

We dream of his bones and our mother's,
deep in a bramble bush of stars,
glowing like boughs in dark water.

Six Bold Turtles

One Tennessee summer I and my brothers
collected a herd of six bold turtles—

not Woolworth gewgaws with painted blooms,
but ringed-back beauties whose high, wide domes

were big as our father's hands. One great slow tortoise
we heaved with both arms into the dirt-edged

washtub. One placed third in a turtle race and one sported
backbone spikes like a stegosaurus.

One was a snapper and one a slider. And one
Eastern box turtle I saw at noon

in school that spring on the muddy grounds
and ran from class in a roaring rain, found

Lochinvar who clumped with an old man's limp,
with his bowed three legs and one smooth stump

worn round as a lake stone. We brought tomatoes,
green and worm-lipped, and crumpled lettuce,

yellowed, but fragrant on turtles'
blunt tongues. When our small garden

grew barren with cold, we carried the troop
to our low, dirt cellar to hibernate deep

in mud of our myths. We vowed after winter
a rescue of dragons, but they remained under

the dark spell of Pluto. Spring brought departure
from reptilian summers. Our folks moved us far northward,

my brothers and me—not heroes, just children—
leaving behind turtles in lost cellars.

Mummy

Home sick from school,
laid out on the daybed,
I tuck the old blanket
under every bone-angle
and tight over my head.

Through the faded red blanket,
rosy light washes thin,
the way light must look
to your muscles, through skin.

But not to your organs,
once cupped in the dark,
then slapped in some pot
to wither and blacken;
while belly and brain pan
hold frankincense and cinnamon.

My mother and grandmother
listen to WATO,
their staticky voices
and clinking coffee cups
echo as our tomb
grows vaguer, more hollow,
lines itself with stone.

Somewhere in the house
with her head on her paws,
a spotted dog naps
and a black cat dream-chases,
her breath all a-chatter.
They're put there for company
in the fragrant hereafter.

They've no sense the air
will dwindle, go dead.
In the backyard, a nuthatch
sends a six note alarm.
No sand dunes to cover us,
just Tennessee River mud.

Over years it will swell
to swaddle our snuggery.
It is rising already;
there's something scary
in the raindrops' tick-tock
dripping from the Chinaberry.

When my brothers come home
and toss down their books,
shocked, but not panicky,
they'll thrust arms to the elbow
in the rising sea of gook,
red and clay-sticky.

When Daddy comes home,
after dark, he'll still find them
with hard hats and shovels
engineers already.
He'll loosen his necktie,
pace out the lie of the land,
white shirt going sweaty.

While a mockingbird, hearing
his preoccupied hum,
will decode and trill
the secret bearing
to these lost rooms of bliss,
this Temple of Ruhlendom.

In the Garden, My Mother Invokes Wordsworth

Wisdom is often nearer when we stoop than when we soar,
she says, pinching peas from vines in the garden,
working mechanisms out in the open
on her bony fingers, with their raised pulleys and blue cords.

She kneels in the garden, pinching peas from vines
and a butterfly dips down to land on one big knuckle
of a hand nothing like Daddy's plump ones. The pulleys and cords
are a bit scary I sometimes think, a bit witchy;

also the butterfly sitting lightly on her big knuckle,
and the spells she casts on plants, on nature.
I'd be scary too, even witchy, if I could,
but I have to yank at the pods with my clumsy fingers.

I cast no spell here, crouching among plants,
listening to the music of peas jumping into her pail,
needing no yanking from her fingers,
while next door my brothers play catch with a wormy corn cob.

They drown out the music of peas hitting Mom's tin pail
with their shouts and the neighbor dog's frantic barking.
As they toss the cob back and forth over its head,
it leaps and leaps, making me jealous.

My thoughts drowned out by the pleasure of their shouts,
oblivious to women's work, our squatting like Indians,
their joy leaping and leaping, makes me jealous.
Not that they wouldn't work too if Daddy were here

who is oblivious to these humdrum divisions of labor,
who is moving us next month to Alaska,
making us leap with joy, all our friends jealous.
He's another magician, I think, my mind day-dreaming off,

next month taking us to Alaska
where icicles drip from eaves like upside-down candles.
Thinking of such magic, day-dreamer that I am,
I ask Mom what will grow in our garden up North,

besides icicles, dripping candle-like from eaves.
Will peas come already frozen on the vine?
I nudge Mom, whose mind must be growing gardens Up North,
day-dreamer herself, and she rises, knocks dirt from her seat,

I reckon, she says, *pee will freeze in mid-air,*
with the dogs and your brothers piddling just anywhere.
She pulls me up, knocks dirt from my seat.
And our backyard snow will be yellow as custard.

My brothers like dogs, piddling everywhere!
But what about us? I ask, giggling
at thoughts of snow the color of custard.
My mom reaches out to touch my cheek,

Who, us women? She laughs, *We don't have*
our working mechanisms right out in the open.
Besides, her fingers are light on my cheek as a butterfly,
wisdom is nearer to those who stoop than those who soar.

Ode to a Parka

For her thirteenth birthday, she got a parka:
a second-hand one, with a quilted Chinese-red lining,
white rabbit skin with worn Indian black, red, and white
rick-rack at the cuffs and the bottom which came
almost to her knees—the right length
to keep your butt warm in Alaskan winters.

Below the rick-rack was a longer fur—gray-brown
with white tips—maybe caribou. Around the hood
bloomed the dark brown hair of the wolverine
which was said not to frost up under your breath.

She didn't dwell much on the animals
that went into her parka. People said
the land was fat with snowshoe rabbits
and last fall she'd watched a herd of caribou
hurtle across the Richardson Highway,
more caribou than you could count.
Both were good meat and it was fine
to do like the Eskimos and use every part.

As for wolverines, they were sneered at,
called "carrion eaters," "vicious," "stinking
to high heaven." No one would eat one.

When she thought of those animals, she called it *love*
and gratitude and some guilt for the wolverine,
a shy beast struggling in the teeth
of a trap hidden in blue snow shadow—
how despised could it be to squander on parka trim?

But she petted her parka, so soft and luscious
and warm, even at twenty below.
It made her want to skim over the snow
with its sharp crust of ice and disappear
into the dark spruce woods: animal
heat inside animal skin almost lifting her.

But she just stood there with the others,
in front of Carr's Market, waiting for the school bus,
tough boys in leather or Army jackets;
graceful girls in long coats that covered
their full skirts and scratchy crinoline
petticoats, bare legs, and snow boots,
carrying in paper bags the ballet slippers
they'd wear in the school halls.

Waiting there, awkward and half-formed,
the secret spirit of her body lost
in the parka's bulk, her legs tingled
and her ears burned, even hooded and scarved.
She hunched her head into her shoulders
to bring the wolverine fur to her nose
where the nostril hairs prickled as they froze
with each in-drawn breath.

Solstice at Hidden Lake

Three girls, naked, poise on jutting rocks.
The youngest shivers, dark hair scarring her back.
She sees the shape of spruce buried in water,
ominous beneath her. The other two fling
themselves out, their splashes echoing.
Alaska midnight, no stars, sun just below the horizon.
Wind footprints the lake. Bray of a loon.
On the other shore, a bull moose wades gently in, swims
the lake's width, pond weed dripping from his beard,
as he nods his massive head. Ratchets himself out.
She breathes willow, algae, skunk cabbage.
She wonders if this is sacrament or mere
dare deviltry. Soul's confidence or body's doubt?
Up on toes now. Brassy water knives her hair.
Three forms blossom in the lake's dark foliage.

Young Lovers at Crow Creek Mine

When they come to the end of the trail
and he spreads his jacket on smooth rock-face
above a thicket of mountain blueberries,
a cloudbank envelopes them in silence.

He spreads his jacket on the boulder
where marmots whistle in fiddlehead fern
that unfurls—through enveloping clouds—
its green flame like smoke off glaciers.

Where marmots whistle in fiddlehead fern,
she stills the ache of her hauling lungs,
aflame with the breath of glaciers.
He says, *The air is very thin.*

Her chest aches from the hike up,
clouds popping water about them.
Delicious, she says of the air as he opens
her jacket like a prayer-book.

Clouds that pop water about them
have crumpled rails to rust in caving galleries.
He ruffles her shirt like the pages of a book
and his lips are cold as snow.

Rails crumble to rust in caving adits.
When she turns her head, she sees a forest of moss.
His lips, like goose-flesh on her skin,
cannot banish the pricking of mosquitos.

Everywhere moss trembles with droplets
and she wonders if that was a bear crashing in the brush.
He shakes away the pricking of mosquitos
and buttons up the front of her shirt. *Could be,*

he laughs, *bears thrashing in thickets*
at the trail's end. This time of year,
zippering up the portal of her jacket, *all nature*
knows the mountains are ripe with berries.

About the Author

Frances Ruhlen McConnel spent her childhood in Oak Ridge, Tennessee, her teens in Anchorage, Alaska, and her young adulthood in Seattle where she received her PhD in Renaissance Literature at the University of Washington. She has two daughters from her first marriage. She moved to Claremont, California in 1973. She is retired from teaching in the Creative Writing Department at the University of California, Riverside. She co-chairs the steering committee that runs the Claremont Public Library's monthly Poetry Reading Series, Fourth Sundays. She has published a chapbook, *White Birches, Black Water,* from the Anchorage fine arts press, Bucket of Type Printery. She has two books of poems: *Gathering Light,* from Pygmalion Press, and *The Direction of Longing,* from Bellowing Ark Press. She edited the anthology of West Coast women poets, *One Step Closer* for Pygmalion Press. Her poems, stories, essays and book reviews have appeared in many journals and anthologies, including *The Iowa Review, The Massachusetts Review, The Nation, The Seattle Review, Pearl, The Seattle Weekly, The New York Times Book Review, Women of the Fourteenth Moon, Bear Flag Republic, The Alaska Quarterly Review, Zyzzyva,* and *The Atlantic Monthly.* In 2004 she won the Oneiros Press Broadside Prize.

www.ingramcontent.com/pod-product-compliance
Lightning Source LLC
LaVergne TN
LVHW091320080426
835510LV00007B/582